IMAGES
of England

AROUND RUBERY
AND THE LICKEY HILLS

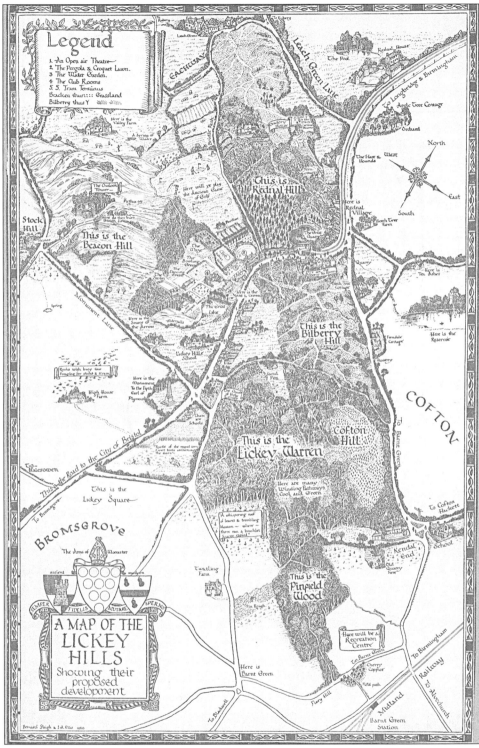

Picture map of the Lickey Hills, published in 1920, showing proposals for recreational development.

2

IMAGES
of England

AROUND RUBERY
AND THE LICKEY HILLS

Compiled by
Martin Hampson

TEMPUS

Tempus Publishing Limited
The Mill, Brimscombe Port,
Stroud, Gloucestershire, GL5 2QG

ISBN 0 7524 2097 6

Typesetting and origination by
Tempus Publishing Limited
Printed in Great Britain by
Midway Clark Printing, Wiltshire

The Lickey Hills, seen from Groveley Lane in the 1960s.

Contents

Acknowledgements

Many thanks to Birmingham Library Services (Local Studies, History and Archives) for allowing me to use their photographs. Special thanks are due to Mr B.W. Gould of Lickey Hills Local History Society, for permission to use the photographs on pp. 14a, 25, 34b, 37a, 38, 39a, 49, 109a, 112, 125b, 126; and to Mr K. Lewis, head master of Hunters Hill School, for the photographs on pp. 90 and 91a. Thanks are also due to Martin Flynn for providing the opportunity to work on this project and for negotiating with the publishers; to Joe McKenna and David Harvey for their help; and to Local Studies staff for welcome technical assistance.

Rubery Hill before the flyover, c. 1910.

Introduction

Sometimes called the 'Hampstead Heath of Birmingham', the Lickey Hills, nine miles to the south of the city, consist of a gently undulating range of woods and heathland, divided by the deep Rednal Gorge, through which descends the old Roman road to Metchley Park. Like Hampstead Heath, the Hills command spectacular views of the city, serve as a popular resort, and are the outcome of an early and far-sighted conservationist campaign.

In medieval times, the whole area consisted of dense woodland, with the occasional tract of heathland or small clearing for a farming settlement. Local place names like the 'ley' of Bartley Green, Frankley and Groveley, suggest the presence of such clearings, as does the 'barnt' of Barnt Green, indicating woodland cleared by burning. Similarly, the name Lickey means 'slab of rock in a forest enclosure'.

Although originally a royal hunting ground, like the adjacent Forest of Feckenham, the Forest of Lickey – first officially recorded as such in 1269 – was confirmed by Edward I to be common land, and again by Lord Windsor who bought the estate in 1682 and resolved an encroachment issue. For centuries a working landscape – with agriculture and latterly quarrying, brickmaking and nailmaking as important industries – the Lickeys were made more accessible to visitors by the opening through the gorge in 1758 of the Birmingham-Worcester stage-coach route. The Rose and Crown remained a popular coaching inn until the opening of an easier coach route through Rubery in 1831.

The opening of the Birmingham-Worcester Canal in 1820 increased the commercial potential of the area, facilitating the transportation of coal and lime from the Black Country and farm produce to Birmingham markets. However it was the opening of Barnt Green station, on the Birmingham-Gloucester Railway Line, in 1840, which marked the crucial turning point. Not only did this provide a much speedier business link than the canal; but the railway enabled Birmingham people to make day trips to the Lickeys with ease. Moreover, Barnt Green, previously a small rural hamlet, developed as a residential suburb, as commuting to the city became a practical proposition. Rednal was to acquire the air of a holiday resort, with guesthouses, tearooms, funfairs and souvenir shops.

Local landowners were, however, steadily reasserting their territorial rights, and gradually enclosing the Lickey Hills, culminating in the fencing round of the Rose and Crown estate in 1883. Fearing the impending development of a long-valued playground, local people formed the Birmingham Association for the Preservation of Open Spaces, which with the strong support of Edward Cadbury and George Cadbury Jnr, was able to purchase Rednal Hill for the city in 1887. The same year, Birmingham Corporation accepted the offer of the lease of Bilberry Hill from Lord Windsor, opening it to the public in 1888 and finally purchasing it in 1913. Between 1904 and 1933, members of the Cadbury family purchased and presented to Birmingham Corporation, Beacon Hill and the large estate belonging to the Rose and Crown. At the sale of the Plymouth estate in 1919 the Corporation bought Cofton Hill and the woods extending to Barnt Green. Thus almost the whole of the wooded area of the Lickeys (474 acres) was preserved as a public open space. The long-standing practice of quarrying for road building also ceased, as the scenic value of the area became increasingly appreciated.

The Cadbury family maintained their interest in the development of the area, shown with the gift of the Bilberry Hill Tearooms in 1904, and the laying out of the municipal golf course in the early 1920s. They also presented to the National Trust the farmland below Beacon Hill and Frankley Beeches, thus preserving the view from the summits and contributing to the inter-linked tracts of countryside forming Birmingham's Green Belt. The opening of a tram service between Birmingham and Rednal in 1924 further increased the development of the area. The whole district reached its peak of tourist popularity in the 1920s, with an estimated 10,000 people waiting in Navigation Street for Lickeys trams by 10.30 a.m. on Easter Monday 1924. The inter-war years saw much housebuilding on the old Rednal House, Leys Farm and Colmers Farm estates – a trend encouraged by the steady expansion of the nearby Austin motor works. Similar housing development occurred in Rubery, particularly after the introduction of a tram service in 1926.

After the end of the Second World War, the Lickeys began to decline as a tourist area, as with increased personal mobility people tended to travel further afield for day trips and holidays. Tourist facilities were gradually reduced through the 1950s and 1960s, so that only one of the original tearooms now remains. In recent years, however, there has been a growing interest in conservation, and the countryside has seen something of a revival in the Lickeys' fortunes, with the establishment of a visitors' centre, the starting of a park ranger service, and long-term plans for re-afforestation and the recycling of timber. The commissioning of some public artworks and the staging of various open-air events have also helped to raise the profile of the area.

As part of the Birmingham countryside, the Lickeys area reflects the variety of the city. Very much reservoir country, it has three canal feeder reservoirs - Cofton, and Upper and Lower Bittell – as well as the reservoirs of Bartley Green and Frankley which receive Birmingham's water supply from the Elan Valley. Rejuvenation of another kind has been provided over the years by institutions serving health, educational or spiritual needs. The former Rubery Hill Hospital met one such need, as did Lickey Grange, former home of Lord Austin, which was for many years a school for the blind. Cropwood, once the home of Barrow Cadbury, was for some time a pioneering open-air school for delicate children, and remains an important special school. The Oratory House at Rednal, built by Cardinal Newman, still survives as a spiritual retreat.

The variety of Birmingham's cultural and industrial heritage is reflected in the names of the famous people associated with the area – Lord Austin, who lived at Lickey Grange and is buried in Lickey churchyard, and whose car factory dominates the view from Bilberry Hill; Jane Loudon, pioneer of gardening for women, whose childhood home was Kitwell House, Bartley Green; Barrow, Edward and George Cadbury junior, who all lived locally at one time, and whose successful chocolate business enabled them to give lavishly to the city and the Hills; Cardinal Newman, a key figure in religious and educational history, who is buried in the grounds of the Oratory House, Rednal; and the writer J.R.R. Tolkien, who lived as a child for several months in the lodge at Oratory House.

Cofton Hackett exemplifies this multifaceted landscape well. The rolling acres of Cofton Park – former Lowhill farmland – are bordered to the south by the Lickey Hills and to the north by what is now the Rover car factory. Earlier industry is represented by Cofton Reservoir, built to feed the Birmingham-Worcester Canal; and national history by the medieval Cofton Hall, where Charles I spent a night during the Civil War. It is the aim of this book to present old and modern images of a landscape that is simultaneously practical and scenic, where a balance is being sought between the requirements of commerce and the needs of conservation.

Martin Hampson
July 2000

One
Rural Past

Dray horses at Cofton Hackett, *c.* 1905.

A chance meeting in Leach Green Lane, at the Rubery end, *c.* 1910.

Leach Green Lane, Rednal, *c.* 1910.

Barnt Green Road, Rednal, before post-war housing development, *c.* 1910.

Scotland Farm, Frankley, 1931.

Walking near Frankley church in the 1920s.

Bringing in the harvest at Frogmill Farm, Frankley, *c.* 1898.

Harvesting at Upper Hill Farm, Frankley in the late 1930s; a transitional scene showing a mix of traditional and modern working dress.

The meet at Frankley church in the 1920s.

New Inns Lane, Frankley, in the early 1970s, shortly before housing developments.

A cottage on Frankley Lane, shortly before its demolition to make way for Bartley Green reservoir works, c. 1930.

Resting by Westminster Farm, near Frankley church in 1925.

Genners Farm, Bartley Green in 1924.

Part of Genners Lane, Bartley Green, seen here in 1924, and now submerged beneath Bartley Green Reservoir.

A house in Kitwell Lane, Bartley Green, 1930.

Moat Farm, Bartley Green, *c.* 1930.

Cromwell Lane, Bartley Green, in 1938.

Haymaking at Bartley Green in the 1920s.

Cottages opposite the schools at Bartley Green in 1937.

The wheelwright's shop, Jiggins Lane, Bartley Green, in the 1920s.

Another view of the wheelwright's shop.

Oxen ploughing at Bartley Green, *c.* 1905.

Bartley Green Mill in the 1920s.

Shenley Court, looking towards Weoley Castle in 1936.

The still rural Barnes Hill, Bartley Green, in 1931, before the construction of Ludstone Road on the right.

Broadhidley Farm, Woodgate, in the 1920s.

Ploughing at Stonehouse Farm, Bartley Green, in the 1920s.

Stonehouse Farm, Bartley Green, in the 1920s. Partly medieval in origin, it is built in two parts, the western-side with thick stone walls, and the eastern-side with small Elizabethan bricks. Believed to have been at one time a watchtower for the nearby Weoley Castle, it was for several centuries occupied by local farmers, one of whom, Isaac Flavel, bought it in 1842. Isaac had made his fortune in California, and he planted the avenue of trees up Stonehouse Hill, built the old California Inn, and named the whole district 'California' in honour of his former state. This part of Bartley Green is still known as California, although the old farmhouse is now a nursery school.

Working in Clapgate Lane, Woodgate, in the 1920s. Though there are now few working farms in the area, something of its rural past is being preserved and interpreted in the Woodgate Valley Country Park, formed in 1984. The visitor centre and urban farm are located on Clapgate Lane.

Two

Landscapes and Landmarks

Walking the dog on a snowbound Beacon Hill in the 1970s.

The Old Rose and Crown, viewed from Bilberry Hill, with Beacon Hill beyond, in 1920. Shortly after, the fields beyond the hotel were converted into a municipal golf course. Both Beacon Hill and the Rose and Crown estate were purchased by the Cadbury family and presented to Birmingham Corporation, to be permanently preserved as a public open space.

A general view of Cofton Hackett and Longbridge, seen from Bilberry Hill, *c.* 1960. Cofton village is in the middle distance, with Cofton Park to the left, and the Longbridge car factory rising in the background.

Another view from Bilberry Hill, taken in 1964, and looking more directly towards Cofton. Cofton Hall can be seen in the foreground, amongst the trees. The Hall was built in the fourteenth century on the site of an earlier manor house. During the Civil War, Charles I is said to have spent a night there (14 May 1645), and following his departure the house was fired to prevent it being used as a Roundhead base. The great hall survived the fire, and the house was partly rebuilt in the early nineteenth century.

A view from Bilberry Hill, *c,* 1960. Cofton Reservoir can be seen in the foreground, and the Upper and Lower Bittell Reservoirs are beyond. Completed by 1836, these reservoirs formed part of the feeder system of the Birmingham and Worcester Canal, which opened in 1820.

Bilberry Hill Tearooms, seen from Rednal Hill, around 1910, with Bilberry Hill rising behind the cafe, and Barnt Green Road and Cofton Reservoir beyond.

Cofton Park, around 1960, with the large Longbridge car factory (now Rover) dominating the northern side. It was founded in 1905 by Herbert Austin, on the site of White and Pike's tin box factory, with initial capital of £15,000. By 1910, the company was employing over 1,000 workers, and in its heyday between 20,000 and 30,000. The firm played a major part in both world wars in the production of military vehicles.

Cofton Park, looking towards the eighteenth-century Lowhill Farm (centre background), in 2000. Originally the farmland to Lowhill Farm, the land became a public park in 1936, forming green 'buffer zone' between the Lickey Hills and the Longbridge car factory. It was temporarily requisitioned for cultivation during the Second World War. Cofton Nursery, which grows plants for Birmingham's parks, was opened by Birmingham Corporation on the Lickey Road side in 1970.

A 1830s engraving by T. Underwood of the 90ft obelisk off Monument Lane, Lickey Hills. It was erected in 1834 to the memory of Other Archer, 6th Earl of Plymouth, a leading local landowner with a seat at nearby Hewell Grange and Colonel-Commandant of the Worcestershire Regiment of Yeomanry Cavalry. He had raised the regiment in 1831, at the request of local magistrates to control possible civil unrest, there being no local police force at the time.

The monument, c. 1905. Its location in a hilltop clearing makes it a prominent landmark for miles around.

Beacon Hill, seen from Chadwich Manor in the 1920s. Commanding a view of ten counties, the hill rises to 937ft. The Cadbury family not only gave Beacon Hill to the city, but also presented the Chadwich estate to the National Trust, thus preserving the view towards Malvern. Being the highest in the Lickey range, the hill originally formed part of a network of beacon sites – hilltop fires being lit in raised iron baskets to warn of an approaching invasion.

The view north-north-east from Beacon Hill, looking over the golf course towards Birmingham, c. 1960.

A view from Rose Hill, looking towards Rednal Hill, *c.* 1905.

Rose Hill, the old Birmingham-Bristol Road, seen from Bilberry Hill, *c.* 1905. The road wa
turnpiked in 1726, and by 1758 a stage-coach service was running between Birmingham an
Worcester. In 1820 the road, whose steepness caused serious problems for coaches, wa
realigned and shortened, but it was gradually supplanted by the new road between Longbridg
and Lydiate Ash which opened in 1831.

Frankley Reservoir during construction, c. 1900. Completed in 1904, the semicircular reservoir receives, filters, and distributes water supplied direct by the aqueduct from the Elan Valley in Wales. Averaging 30-35ft in depth, it has a holding capacity of 200 million gallons.

Bartley Green Reservoir during construction in the late 1920s. Completed in 1930, it provides an additional storage capacity of 500 million gallons.

Frankley Beeches seen from across Bartley Green Reservoir in the 1930s.

Frankley Beeches in the 1970s. This wooded hill, rising to a height of 795ft, was presented by the Cadbury family to the National Trust in 1930. The largest of the beech trees is said to have been felled by Gladstone in 1880; and from 1921 to 1924 a pioneering radio-receiving station stood on the hill, receiving signals from Marconi's station in Cornwall. Close by is a small plantation which supplies new trees when old ones die. The farmland immediately around the trees is to be preserved so as to safeguard the view.

The view from Frankley Beeches in 1966, looking towards Birmingham over Frankley and Bartley Green Reservoirs.

Smart's brickworks, California, 1941. For many years in the nineteenth century the brickworks, along with the associated claypits, were the only alternative industry to nailmaking or farming in the Bartley Green area. Alongside the brickworks ran a canal, which was an arm linking the Worcester-Birmingham Canal with the network of Black Country canals at Halesowen. In the background, on the left, may be seen the Stonehouse Inn, with the gable end of Stonehouse Farm beyond the trees to the right. The site is now a recreation ground.

Egghill Lane, near Frankley Beeches, at the Frankley/Longbridge boundary, 1944.

The seventeenth-century Rubery Farm, on Rubery Lane, was a reminder of Rubery's early origins. 'Robery' (meaning 'rough hills') was mentioned in 1649, but the farm, seen here in 1951, was demolished around 1970.

Leach Green Lane seen from Rubery Quarry, *c.* 1920. Quarrying was a major industry in Rubery through the nineteenth and early twentieth centuries; a claypit also provided raw material for a flourishing brickworks.

Climbing the old quarry face in 1983. Several physical reminders of the quarrying remain among the modern housing, as well as the names Cliff Rock Road and Quarry Walk.

The flyover at Rubery, seen from Rubery Hill in the 1970s. The Rubery bypass, completed in 1962, has relieved New Road of through-motorway traffic; but has tended to separate the residential from the business district.

The Cock Inn, Rubery, in the early 1970s, in a still predominantly rural setting, shortly before major housing developments in the area.

New Inns Lane, Frankley, seen at the start of the housing developments of the mid-1970s.

A view over Woodgate Valley in 1970, showing an essentially transitional landscape.

A still rural stretch of Woodgate Valley, in 1982, shortly before its designation as a country park. In a city council initiative to preserve 450 acres of natural countryside and old farmland, footpaths and bridleways were constructed, and repairs made to bridges, weirs and stepping stones. Thousands of new trees were planted, and many wild flowers grown in the city's nurseries at Cofton were reintroduced into the valley. There are now facilities for pony trekking and guided tours, as well as educational work for children. Footpaths link Woodgate Valley to the Green Belt area via Bartley Green Reservoir and Frankley Beeches.

Three
Street Scenes

Hewell Road, Barnt Green's main street, *c.* 1900.

Lickey Road before development, looking towards Birmingham, *c.* 1910. The Rednal House estate is on the left, and the Lowhill Farm estate on the right. While the Lowhill farmland (now Cofton Park) remains a public open space, the Rednal House estate was progressively built up in the inter-war period, housing developments being completed by the 1950s. The hedge on the left, just beyond Leach Green Lane, is said to be at least 700 years old and marks the boundary of the original Roman road. The presence of telegraph poles reminds us that a phone service had been available in Rednal since the opening of the Barnt Green exchange in 1899; but it was little used until the opening of the Rubery exchange in 1920, and as late as 1925 there were still only fifteen Rednal subscribers.

Rednal tram terminus, *c.* 1950. First mentioned as 'Wreodanhale' as early as 780, and as 'Rednall' by 1594, the name means 'meadow at the corner of the thicket' – a clear reference to the well-wooded Lickeys terrain. As the tram 'railhead' for the Lickey Hills (which can be seen in the background), it still retained something of a village atmosphere, although it had formed part of Birmingham since 1911.

Rednal village, with the tram service and its tracks now gone, *c.* 1960. Although traditional tourist facilities such as tearooms, funfairs and souvenir shops were by this time much diminished, the presence of a large amusement arcade beyond the parked cars shows Rednal's adaptability to changing needs. Lickey Road, curving to the right, leads past the Hare and Hounds towards Birmingham.

RDL.65. THE VILLAGE. REDNAL.

Another 1960s view of Rednal, looking the opposite way towards Barnt Green, with the amusement arcade on the right and lavish facilities for bus passengers on the left.

Barnt Green Road, Rednal, looking towards the junction with Lickey Road, Rose Hill and Groveley Lane (Four Ways), around 1910. The cottages on the left, with Rednal Hill in the background, were situated on Rose Hill. They have been removed for road widening, as have the cottages at the junction straight ahead, where a roundabout now dominates the scene.

Looking down Lickey Road, Rednal, towards Barnt Green, *c.* 1910. This part of the village now presents a rather less sylvan appearance, with the road widened and the view opened out on the left.

The lower slope of Rose Hill just round the corner, seen here in 2000 as it approaches the Old Rose and Crown. This view has changed little in general appearance for several generations.

Houses on the Rednal House estate, seen in 1952, shortly after completion. Major housing developments occurred in Rednal following the opening of the tram service to Birmingham in 1924, facilitating commuting as well as tourism. Most of the Rednal Triangle – the area between Leach Green Lane, Lickey Road and Bristol Road South – was built up in the inter-war period and immediately after the end of the Second World War. Starting as an ambitious private scheme, the development shown here – along with the adjacent Leys Farm and Colmers Farm estates – was completed by Birmingham City Council.

Hewell Road, Barnt Green, c. 1910. Although the Plymouth family had originally encouraged the building of Barnt Green station for the convenience of their tenant farmers, by the 1880s, with the release of Plymouth land for housing, many more people were beginning to appreciate this amenity. Houses began to be built near the station, and a recognisable village centre was formed, with shops, pubs and a temperance hotel, where previously there had been only a scattered rural hamlet. Barnt Green is thus a railway village, a purpose-built commuter suburb, whose main shopping street retains something of its Victorian cottage scale to this day.

New Road, Rubery, around 1905, with the road surface very much that of horse-drawn transport, and the Congregational chapel and adjacent community hall on the right. Close to the foot of Cock Hill Lane, it was erected as a Methodist chapel in 1841; but was used by the Congregationalists from 1851 until its destruction by fire in 1959. The flyover of the bypass now obstructs such an open vista.

The New Rose and Crown and New Road, Rubery, c. 1915. At this time, the tram service from Birmingham ran only as far as Selly Oak, and an open-topped bus (shown here) completed the journey to Rubery.

The New Rose and Crown, Rubery, *c*. 1915. The pub is so called because it supplanted the Rose and Crown at Rednal as the area's coaching inn once the new stagecoach route from Longbridge to Bromsgrove was opened through Rubery in 1831. Although the coaching trade steadily declined following the opening of the Birmingham-Gloucester Railway in 1840, the inn still maintained stables at the turn of the century, hiring out horse-drawn vehicles to convey visitors round the Lickey Hills.

New Road, Rubery's main street, around 1910 when it was still predominantly residential in character. Like the New Rose and Crown, its name reflects the diversion of the stagecoach route from Rose Hill, Rednal, to Rubery in 1831. New Road was originally part of Bristol Road South which passed through Rubery, though the building of the bypass in 1962 has now relieved it of that role.

New Road, Rubery, seen from the Plough Inn, c. 1910. The opening of the new road to Bromsgrove in 1831 led to the rapid development of the area, which had previously been a small farming and nailmaking community – an impact not dissimilar from that of the railway at Barnt Green. Like Hewell Road, Barnt Green, New Road is very much a planned street, much of it built simultaneously in the late nineteenth century. By 1900, Rubery had four inns (three with their own stables), as well as two blacksmiths, several shops, large quarries, a claypit and a brickworks. New Road retains something of its original character, although the bypass has now cut off the Plough from the rest of the street.

The shop of A. Grosvenor, chemist and optician, New Road, Rubery, c. 1915.

Shopping at Newman Way, Rubery, in 1963. The Valley Farm estate, on the lower slopes of Beacon Hill, was built by Birmingham Corporation, although it lies outside the city's boundaries. Following a lottery in 1962, Birmingham-born couples under thirty were selected to buy houses here.

Rubery bypass, opened in 1962, seen here in the 1970s.

Bartley Green village in 1933, looking down Adams Hill. Bartley Green was a very old settlement, being mentioned in the Domesday Book as 'Berchelai', meaning 'the clearing in the birch trees'. It was for centuries a small agricultural village, retaining several working farms even in the inter-war period. The farms were mostly small, and from the eighteenth century onwards incomes were supplemented by nailmaking, and later by brickmaking and the associated claypit workings. The village became part of Birmingham in 1911.

Bartley Green village in 1937, still retaining a close-knit centre. Major change came only after the end of the Second World War, with the building in the early 1950s of a large housing estate to accommodate relocated city dwellers, and the consequent escalation of road traffic.

Bartley Green village, 1937, looking towards Northfield. Between the First and Second World wars, the area became something of a local tourist attraction, as people from the inner-city suburbs came by bus (which terminated at this point) to see the reservoir, and picnic in the bluebell woods.

Bartley Green village, showing the bus terminus and Adams Hill, in the 1930s. Bartley Green was never served by trams; but enjoyed a regular bus service to Birmingham from 1923. There was a coffee shop at the terminus where commuters used to change their shoes or wellingtons and leave them safe at the cafe until they returned from work. This was a welcome amenity, since many roads remained unmade into the 1950s.

Bartley Green school and fire station, seen in 1931. On the right is the gateway to the original St Michael's church. The village school was first opened in 1840 as a Sunday school, becoming a day school in 1845, and by 1846 it had a permanent schoolmistress. Following the 1870 Education Act, the school was rebuilt, though it still consisted of only a single room, with a partition, warmed by a coke stove. By this time, there were 165 pupils, but still only one teacher. Additional buildings were erected in 1884. Older residents remember the 'fire engine' being a handcart with buckets. All the buildings in the picture were demolished for road widening.

Bartley Green, alongside the recently completed reservoir, in 1931.

Housing in Woodgate Valley, in 1982. This was part of the major expansion of the original Bartley Green estate, which was developed intensively in the 1960s and 1970s.

Four
The Lickey Hills

Rose Hill, looking towards Bilberry Hill Tearooms, with the quarry on the left, *c.* 1910.

George Cadbury Jnr, (1878-1957), son of the founder of Bournville, who was himself a director of the chocolate company for forty-four years, and shared his father's interests in adult education, town planning and housing reform. As a city councillor, he played a major part in the development of council estates in the inter-war period. For some years, he owned a house on the Lickeys (Beaconwood), and was one of the leading figures in the campaign to preserve the hills as a public amenity.

Edward Cadbury, (1873-1948), brother of George Cadbury Jnr, was also a director of the family firm, and followed his father as a director of the *Daily News*. He was a notable benefactor, particularly in the field of higher education, founding the Selly Oak College Library, as well as the Chair of Theology, St Francis Hall, and Edward Cadbury lecture series at Birmingham University. A campaigner for old age pensions and women's rights in industry, he too lived for a time on the Lickeys, and successfully fought with his brother for their preservation.

The Lickey Hills, viewed from Cofton Park, around 1920, showing the park still as farmland and Rednal as still a predominantly rural village.

Cofton Green, just below the previous viewpoint, c. 1910. This picture shows the kind of transport used around the Lickeys at this time.

Cofton Cottage, at Cofton Green, c. 1920. The cottage was one of Rednal's most popular souvenir shops, with an inviting roadside stall.

Four Ways, Rednal, c. 1907. Visitors are being conveyed by carriage around the hills, with Barnt Green Road to the left and Rose Hill to the right. The centre of this scene is now occupied by a traffic roundabout.

A crowd of visitors flocking along the same stretch of Rose Hill, c. 1910. They are in no way deterred by the quarry which had for so long provided road making materials for the area. This is a graphic illustration of the popularity of the Lickeys early in the twentieth century, even before the area had been fully conserved for future generations. An estimated 20,000 people visited the hills one Bank Holiday in 1919.

The main flight of steps up Bilberry Hill, seen from Rose Hill, c. 1910. Bilberry Hill was leased by Birmingham Corporation from Lord Windsor in 1889, and purchased outright in 1913. The comparative nakedness of the hill before later tree-planting is very obvious.

Bilberry Hill, Lickeys.

A closer view of the steps up Bilberry Hill, *c.* 1910. Such an open view is no longer possible, since the steps are now shaded by close-growing mature trees.

The summit of Bilberry Hill, *c.* 1905.

Another view of Bilberry Hill summit, around 1905, exemplifying the landscape characterised by Elihu Burritt as 'perfectly Scotch in cut and clothing'. Bilberry Hill is the moorland tract of the Lickey range, with quartzite boulders over 500 million years old rising from the gently undulating acres of heather, gorse and bracken, interspersed with clusters of Scots pines. It is notable for the annual profusion of bilberries from which it takes its name, and for the spectacular open views northwards towards Birmingham.

Bilberry Hill around 1930, showing a clearing full of heather and bilberry bushes, with one of the hill's many viewpoint seats.

The drive in the wood at Lickey Warren, seen in the 1920s. Lickey Warren, adjacent to Bilberry Hill, has a more park-like aspect, particularly in the vicinity of Warren Lane, where an arboretum, children's playground and visitor centre are now situated. In former years, tearooms and a permanent funfair were sited here.

Cofton Woods in the 1930s. Lying between Bilberry Hill and Barnt Green, they were bought by Birmingham Corporation in 1919, at the sale of the Earl of Plymouth's estate. Different again in character from the other hills, they consist of dense deciduous and coniferous woodland, divided by a small valley, and interspersed with winding paths and streams, and – befits ancient woodland – thickly carpeted with bluebells in the spring.

A panoramic view from beside a Scots pine on Bilberry Hill includes Cofton Hackett village in the foreground, with Cofton Park and the Longbridge car factory (recognised by the large white block) in the middle distance, and the city of Birmingham beyond. Taken in 1972, this photograph clearly shows the close intermingling of industrial and rural scenes that characterises the area.

Rose Cottage Tearooms, Rednal, one of a number of similar establishments (several called Rose Cottage) that operated around this time (1910) in the Lickeys area. Some cafes simply provided pots of tea, others full meals, and a few accommodation as well. Only one of the original tearooms now remains, on the golf course behind the Old Rose and Crown.

The quarry in Rednal Gorge, *c.* 1910. Quarrying for road making and building material was prevalent throughout the Rubery and Rednal areas during the nineteenth and early twentieth century. The quarries at Rednal Hill and Bilberry Hill were particularly valued for their yield of hard-core for roads, and the hills would in all probability have been quarried away had no conservationists intervened around this time.

Another view of the quarry in Rednal Gorge, *c.* 1910. This views shows how much of Rednal Hill had already been quarried away. As at Malvern however – another hill area once threatened by quarrying – careful tree-planting is restoring a greener and more natural appearance to the hillside.

A view from Bilberry Hill, c. 1910. This views looks over the Old Rose and Crown and up Rose Hill towards Monument Lane, which runs to the right along the skyline towards Beacon Hill. Rose Hill, a former Roman road and medieval saltway, became a toll road in 1726, and by 1758 a regular stagecoach service was running between Birmingham and Worcester, with the Rose and Crown serving as a popular coaching inn. There were operating problems from the start; highwaymen frequented the route, and the hill was so steep that the coaches needed iron drags on their wheels. Although abandoned as a coaching route after the opening of the new road through Rubery in 1831, Rose Hill remained popular for local travel to Bromsgrove. The last tolls were collected here in 1872.

The traffic island at Four Ways, Rednal, in the 1960s. The centre of the village is up the slope straight ahead, and the Chalet Club (now the Poacher's Pocket pub) in the foreground. For Birmingham visitors, this is regarded as the gateway to the Lickeys.

The Bilberry Hill Tearooms and Rose Hill, at the entrance to Rednal Gorge, *c.* 1930.

The Bilberry Hill Tearooms, seen from Rednal Hill, *c.* 1910. They were originally Cadbur company property; but were given to the city by Mr and Mrs Barrow Cadbury in 1904. For man years they were a leading venue for visitors to the Lickeys, with their large hall for partie concerts and dances, as well as smaller refreshment rooms.

Bilberry Hill Tearooms, around 1905, showing the remains of quarry workings in the foreground and pleasure gardens beyond the fence. The tearooms became a youth training centre in 1960.

The garden at the tearooms, c. 1905.

Another popular venue was the York Jones Tearoom and Pleasure Garden on Cofton Hil c. 1950.

The Cofton Wood Tearoom, c. 1950.

York Jones cafe advertisements, 1924.

Bradmore's Guide to the Lickey Hills was published in 1924, shortly after the hills were fully opened to the public, when they were enjoying their greatest period of popularity.

The Old Rose and Crown, in the late 1880s, shortly after it had been rebuilt by Alfred Wenham, a Birmingham accountant who also founded Rednal Evangelical church, and who had purchased the estate following the closure of the old inn. Wenham called his new house 'Lickey Hills' which became a centre for evangelical meetings, and it was only after his departure that a purpose-built church was erected. He elaborately landscaped the grounds, channelling the River Arrow into a spectacular series of pools and cascades. It was his fencing round of the estate that alerted conservationists to the steady loss of common land throughout the area.

Elihu Burritt, the American consul to Birmingham, 1865-1869, paid an enthusiastic tribute to the Lickey Hills in his *Walks in the Black Country and its Green Borderland* (1868). He first visited the area in June 1846, at the start of a walking tour of England, staying at the Old Rose and Crown, which he visited again twenty-one years later.

The grounds of the Old Rose and Crown, showing the steadily maturing landscaping, *c.* 1905

A bank of daffodils just behind the Old Rose and Crown overlook the lake which was created by damming the River Arrow, *c.* 1930.

A general view over the lake towards the hotel and Rednal Hill, in 1972.

In 2000 the lake remains remarkably unchanged, which can be seen in this view looking towards the golf course and Beacon Hill.

Beacon Hill, c. 1960. Although mostly well-wooded, the hill has an open grassy summit commanding wide-ranging views of the Malverns, Rubery, Frankley and Birmingham.

The Outlook Tower.

The Outlook Tower on Beacon Hill, from *Bradmore's Guide to the Lickey Hills* (1924). Built close to the site where the original beacon fires were lit, it contained a raised circular panoramic map of the area, indicating all the most prominent landmarks. The tower has been recently rebuilt.

A view from Beacon Hill, looking over the golf course towards Rednal Hill, *c.* 1960.

Skiing on the Lickeys in 1965.

Forestry work on the Lickeys in 1965. The hills remain a working forest, with much timber used for fencing, steps, seats and picnic tables in the Lickeys themselves, as well as meeting the needs of other Birmingham parks. Ancient crafts such as coppicing are being revived, while surplus Christmas trees are given to schools and hospitals. Felled trees are systematically replaced, and stretches of woodland are rejuvenated when required, as on Beacon Hill where diseased conifers have been replaced by a mixture of oaks and softwoods, (partly financed by timber sales).

Although the Lickey Hills are no longer the major tourist attraction that they were in the early part of the twentieth century, a growing interest in the countryside and conservation generally, has led to a demand for better facilities for visitors. The opening of the Visitors' Centre in 1990, offering an interpretative exhibition, refreshments and gift shop, marked the trend towards a higher public profile. School party visits are encouraged, and there are occasional events such as forestry demonstrations, guided tours of the hills, and seasonal celebrations. The centre is shown here in 2000, with the picnic area and children's playground in the foreground.

'The Spirit of the Woods' is one of a number of wooden public artworks scattered round the hills, which have appeared in recent years, some in secluded and unexpected places, and all referring in some way to the natural environment. This sculpture, seen in 2000, is situated in the recreation ground in front of the Visitors' Centre.

Five
Houses and Institutions

Two contemporary institutions: Lickey Elementary Schools (1855) and Holy Trinity church, Lickey (1856), shown around 1910.

St Michael's church, Cofton Hackett, was built around 1330, to serve as a chapel for the adjacent Cofton Hall, the manor house of the Leycesters, and later of the Jolliffes and the Earls of Plymouth. The register dates back to 1550, showing that by that time a wider community was being served. The church, seen here in 1905, was extensively restored by Henry Day in 1861, and acquired its first incumbent in 1880. The name 'Cofton' means 'settlement in a recess in a hill'. The village appeared as 'Costune' in the Domesday Book, and William Hacket held the manor in 1166.

The timber porch of St Michael's church, Cofton Hackett, in 1905. The porch and bell turret, probably dating from the fifteenth century, survived the Victorian restoration, as did the various monuments to the Leycesters and Jolliffes.

A corner of the fourteenth-century great hall of the adjacent manor house, Cofton Hall, *c.* 1910. Part of the, massive hammer-beamed roof can be seen. Most of the original building was destroyed by fire on 15 May 1645, on the orders of Charles I who had spent the night there with his friend Thomas Jolliffe, and did not wish the Hall to be used as a Parliamentarian base. Cofton Hall was partly rebuilt in the early nineteenth century, but the great hall, its finest surviving part, was retained.

The Oratory Retreat House, Rednal, c. 1910. This view gives a clear idea of its secluded, steep and well-wooded site. It was built by Cardinal Newman in 1854 as a retreat for members of his order, the Oratory of St Philip Neri, Edgbaston, and the grounds include a cemetery for the priests. Newman used the house regularly as a weekend retreat, keeping there a library of serious recreational reading. He also paid shorter visits, walking from Edgbaston and back in a single day. He is now buried alongside fellow priests in the grounds. The writer J.R.R. Tolkien, who was at one time a pupil at the Oratory School, stayed with his mother during her final illness, (1903-1904), at the Lodge in the grounds of Oratory House, which still serves as a spiritual retreat.

John Henry Newman (1801-1890), a religious poet and educationalist as well as a theologian, was a founding father of the Oxford Movement and a famous convert to Catholicism. He came to Birmingham in 1849, establishing the Oratory of St Philip Neri which was a community of priests, with an adjacent school, at Hagley Road, Edgbaston. He and his order were much involved in helping the poor of central Birmingham, and Newman personally ensured that the needy in Rednal always had adequate supplies of coal. The church of the Immaculate Conception, adjoining the Oratory, was built in 1903-1909 as his memorial.

Newman died on 11 August 1890, and was buried in the grounds of the Oratory Retreat House, Rednal.

Holy Trinity church, Lickey village, *c.* 1890. The building was designed by Henry Day in the Early English style, and was completed in 1856 at a cost of £3,000.

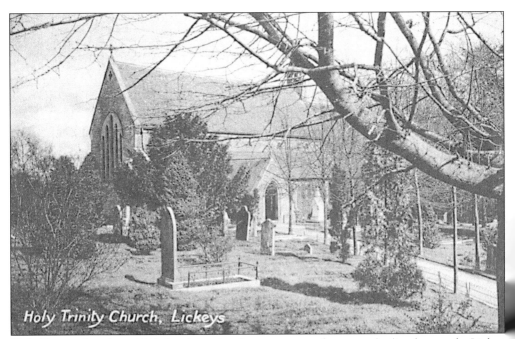

Holy Trinity church, *c.* 1910. Lord Austin, the motor manufacturer, who lived at nearby Lickey Grange, attended this church and is buried in the churchyard.

Rednal Library, on Leach Green Lane, in 1913. The library was opened on 12 June 1909, funds being provided by Andrew Carnegie, and purchase money for the site being given by Edward Cadbury and George Cadbury Jnr.

The reading room at Rednal Library, in 1913. At this time, the library opened 9 a.m.-9 p.m. Monday-Saturday, with the main room displaying magazines and newspapers (the latter with the racing results pasted over). Books were all on closed access, and were issued 7 p.m.-9 p.m. Wednesday, and 3 p.m.-4 p.m. Saturday from a small room. There were two tickets available, one for fiction and one for non-fiction. Open access was not introduced until the 1930s. The library was recently closed, and successfully converted to residential accommodation

A visit of the Green Howards Regiment to Colmers Farm School, Rednal in 1975. The school, named after a former farm in the area, was built in 1940, and was an innovative building in its day.

Meeting the Green Howards' regimental mascot at Colmers Farm School in 1975.

A girls' football team at Colmers Farm School in 1972.

Colmers Farm School trip to London Zoo in 1972.

Lickey Grange, the former home of Lord Austin, in 1947, after its conversion to a school for the blind – an appropriate role in view of Lord Austin's keen support of medical charities. Bought by Birmingham Royal Institution for the Blind in 1943, and extended by them in 1948 and 1951, it served initially as the junior annexe to their main building in Carpenter Road, Edgbaston. In 1953, however, following the acquisition of the Carpenter Road premises by the BBC, the whole school was transferred to Lickey Grange.

Lord and Lady Austin, photographed in 1936. Herbert Austin (1866-1941) was born at Little Missenden, Buckinghamshire; he served his engineering apprenticeship in Australia and married an Australian, Helen Dron. Returning to England in 1893, he designed and produced his first car in 1895, starting the Austin Company at Longbridge in 1905. During his lifetime, the site grew from 2.5 acres to 220 acres. On his elevation to the peerage, he said of his wife, 'In everything I have done she has stood by me, giving me courage to go on'. His factory (now Rover) faces the Lickey Hills across Cofton Park. During his life he was closely associated with the Lickey Hills; he test-drove the first Austin car on the hills, lived there for many years, and he and his wife are buried in Lickey churchyard.

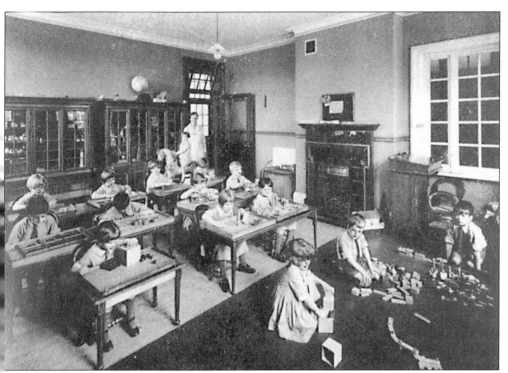

A classroom at Lickey Grange in 1947.

A picnic in the grounds of Lickey Grange, 1947. Visitors to the school commented on its happy atmosphere, pointing out that, although the blind pupils could not see the panoramic views towards Malvern, they clearly sensed them, and benefited from the pure, fresh air and wide open aspect of the estate. The school was recently closed, and the house and grounds converted to residential accommodation.

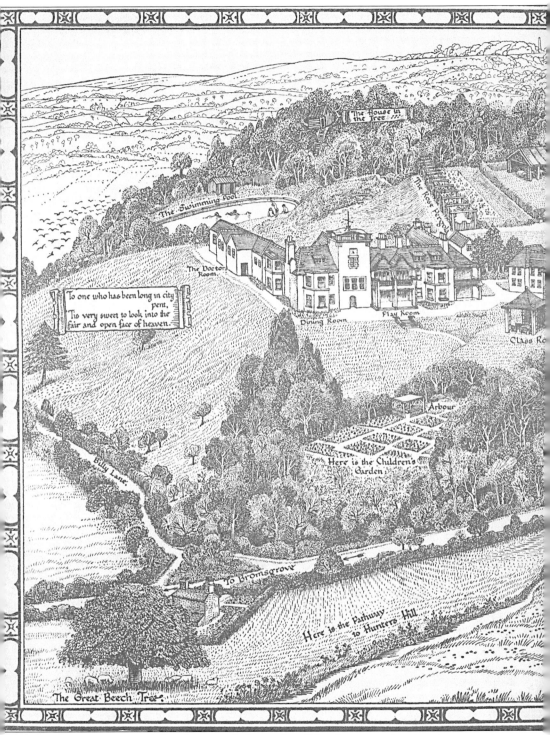

The labels on the map read:

The House in the Tree

The Rose Pergola

The Swimming Pool

The Doctor's Room

Play Room

Dining Room

Class Ro[om]

To one who has been long in city pent, 'Tis very sweet to look into the fair and open face of heaven.

Arbour

Here is the Children's Garden

Billy Lane.

To Bromsgrove

Here is the Pathway to Hunters Hill

The Great Beech Tree.

A picture map of the Cropwood Open Air School estate, showing its many innovator features. The map was published to mark its opening in 1922. Cropwood was the former hom[e] of Barrow and Geraldine Cadbury, originally built by them in 1906, as a holiday home. Whe[n]

CROPWOOD
OPEN AIR
SCHOOL
❖ ❖ ❖
Blackwell near Bromsgrove
In 75 acres of Ground

Go out, children & from the city
Sing out children, as the little
thrushes do
Pluck your handfuls of the meadow
cowslips pretty
Laugh aloud, and feel your fingers
let them through

Here are Pigsties

The Childrens Playing Lawn

Arbour

The Tennis Court

The Orchard

The Vegetable Garden

The Stables

To Barnt Green

The Lodge

I saw a crowd
A host of golden daffodils
Fluttering and dancing in the
breeze—
And then my heart with pleasure
Fills
And dances with the daffodils

Here is the Shelter and
Rosemary Cottage

Vegetable Garden

Public playing Field

The Pool

...heir son Paul became delicate, the house was adapted so that there were two open-air
...edrooms. Paul's obvious benefit from this open-air regime inspired his parents to convert the
...ouse into a school for delicate children.

Cropwood Open Air School in the 1950s, showing lessons in progress. Whereas Uffculme, at Moseley, Barrow Cadbury's other open-air school, took day pupils, Cropwood was residential, concentrating in its early years on delicate children from inner-city homes. The secluded, well wooded, elevated setting was considered a major factor in their physical rejuvenation. In spite of its bracing reputation – particularly in winter, when the children sat writing in their overcoats – most pupils in fact benefited from the regular fresh air, exercise and wholesome food. Long country walks, gardening and physical education alternated with regular rest periods in the grounds.

An open-air class at Cropwood in 1955. Cropwood's intake alternated at first between boys and girls; but following the opening of the adjacent Hunters Hill School in 1933, Cropwood took girls and Hunters Hill took boys. Hunters Hill officially absorbed Cropwood in 1981, and remains an important special school, though no longer 'open-air'.

Barrow Cadbury (1862-1958) was for some years, like his cousins Edward Cadbury and George Cadbury Jnr, a director of the family firm, and also a resident on the Lickey Hills. While sharing the long-standing Cadbury concern with adult education, he and his wife, Geraldine, were particularly interested in the welfare of young people. They built a remand home at Erdington, a model juvenile court, and founded special schools for delicate children at Uffculme and Cropwood. They maintained a close personal interest in both schools, from the smallest details of furnishing and equipment, to all aspects of the curriculum.

St Andrew's church, Barnt Green, c. 1930. The building was designed by A.S. Dixon and buil
1909-1914. The building of a parish church at this time reflects the effect that the railway hac
had on local residential development, since in the 1851 census the population had beer
only forty-six.

The Barnt Green Inn, seen here in 2000, dates from around 1602, though there were many lat
extensions and alterations. It was formerly the home of the land agent to the Earls of Plymou
(the Windsor-Clive family) of Hewell Grange.

Following the release of building land on the Plymouth estate, and the consequent development of Barnt Green village from the 1880s onwards, the kind of properties built became increasingly ambitious, as wealthy Birmingham businessmen recognised the feasibility of commuting from the Lickeys. By 1900, the first large houses were appearing on the wooded slopes of the hills, of which Stretton Croft (seen here in 1920) was one.

Brook House, seen in 1918, was another large commuter home. Many of these mansions, in extensive wooded grounds, still survive, and many others – albeit on a more modest scale – are still being built.

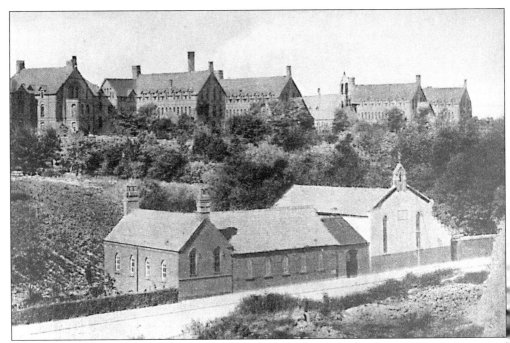

Rubery Hill Hospital, *c.* 1915. Completed by Martin and Chamberlain in 1882 at a cost of £140,000, it was built to provide relief for the first Birmingham asylum at Winson Green. The new hospital accommodated 409 male and 408 female patients.

Hollymoor Annexe, whose opening by the Lord Mayor on 6 May 1905 is pictured here, accommodated a further 302 male and 302 female patients. During the First World War Rubery Hill was adapted and equipped for sick and wounded soldiers. There was much reconstruction after the war, including the building of a male nurses' home.

The main entrance and chapel at Hollymoor, in 1955. Following the closure of the hospital, most of the buildings on the site have been demolished; but the prominent tower with its green cupola has been retained.

Rubery Hill Hospital in 1926, showing patients relaxing in the extensive park-like grounds. At present, the park is being redeveloped for residential and commercial use.

The Congregational church hall, Rubery, after its destruction by fire in 1959. It stood just in front of Rubery Hill Hospital.

THE NEW CONGREGATIONAL CHAPEL : RUBERY.

The new Congregational church at Rubery, in the late 1960s.

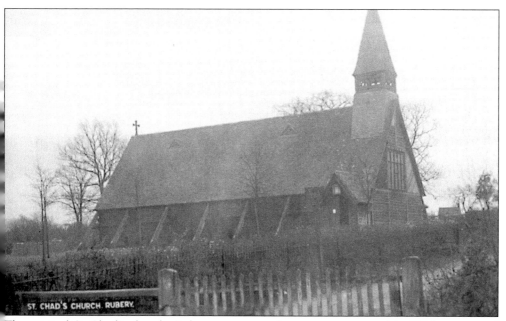

The original St Chad's church, Rubery, was a wooden structure, erected in 1895 at a cost of £700 and seating 200 persons. It is seen here around 1910.

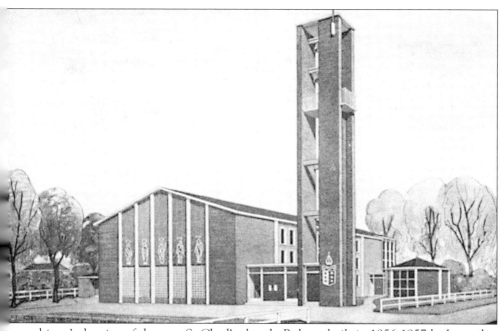

An architect's drawing of the new St Chad's church, Rubery, built in 1956-1957 by Lavender, Twentyman & Percy. Prominent features include the detached square brick campanile and an octagonal chapel, linked on the right of the altar, to the main body of the church

St Leonard's church, Frankley, seen here in an engraving of 1812, was originally the chape
to Frankley Manor, which in 1642 was destroyed by Royalists (like Cofton Hall) to preven
its use as a Roundhead base. Originally a medieval church, in the Early English style, with
registers dating from 1598, its short tower was built in 1751 with stones salvaged from th
ruined manor. The church was restored in 1885, and again in 1931, (following a fire). Th
village, which remained small and semi-rural until major developments in the 1970s, wa
named 'Franchelie' (meaning 'Franca's clearing') in the Domesday Book. It was absorbed b
the city of Birmingham in 1995.

St Leonard's, Frankley, in the 1920s. The church contains several monuments to the Lyttelton family who were for centuries lords of the manor.

The interior of Frankley church, c. 1890. It is seen here soon after the major restoration by Frederick Preedy, when the previously plastered wagon roof – an original Perpendicular feature – was uncovered.

St Michael's church, Bartley Green, in 1933. The original church, at the junction of Field Lane and Jiggins Lane, was built by Isaac Newry in 1838, then enlarged in 1876 to form a T-shaped plan. It was of a simple Gothic style in red brick with sandstone dressings.

The interior of St Michael's, again in the 1930s, showing the attractive queen-post roo Although the original churchyard survives, the church itself was replaced in the late 1960s b a more modern building further down the lane.

Bartley Green Library – like Rednal Library a Carnegie gift – was built in 1905 on land given by Henry Adkins. At one time, in order to stimulate demand, the book stocks of Rednal and Bartley Green Libraries were rotated. This picture dates from 1913.

The reading room at Bartley Green Library in 1913, showing the open newspapers on sloping shelves, and the periodicals neatly arranged along the refectory-style table with its hard upright wooden seats. As at Rednal Library, the book stock was on closed access at this time.

Another view of the reading room in 1913, showing the gas lighting and a number of admonitory notices. Also characteristic of the time are the high-positioned windows which strictly limited the view outside, the heavy glazed wooden screen, and the roll-up map, which would all be familiar features to schoolchildren of the day.

Kitwell House, Bartley Green, in 1951, shortly before its demolition. This was the childhood home of Jane Loudon.

Jane Loudon, nee Webb (1807-1858), pioneering botanist and horticulturist, was born in Edgbaston, but grew up at Kitwell House, Bartley Green, where the then rural environment no doubt encouraged her lifelong interest in plants. In September 1830 she married the landscape gardener and architect John Claudius Loudon, who was a prolific author as well as a notable practitioner, and is remembered locally as the designer of Birmingham's Botanical Gardens. For many years, Jane Loudon worked as her husband's secretary, and from 1840 began to publish botanical and horticultural works in her own right. The work of the Loudons was innovative in that it was aimed at the small amateur gardener as well as the professional.

Mrs. LOUDON's

GARDENING

FOR

LADIES.

Instructions in gardening for ladies (1840) was one of a series of popular botanical and horticultural works written by Jane Loudon in the 1840s. A pioneer of women gardeners, she paved the way for famous garden designers such as Gertrude Jekyll and Vita Sackville-West.

Six

Transport

Kendal End, Barnt Green, in 1926.

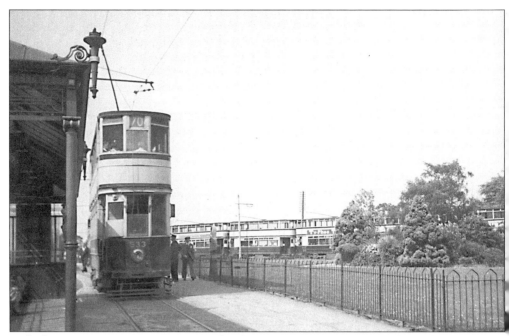

Rednal tram terminus, seen in 1952, shortly before closure. The Bristol Road tram service originally extended only as far as Selly Oak, both Rubery and Rednal being served by connecting bus services from 1913. The tram service was extended from Selly Oak, to the Longbridge car factory on 17 December 1923, and on to Rednal on 14 April 1924. The new through-service from the city became immediately popular with residents and visitors alike. The terminus, later used by buses, was just over the Birmingham boundary, in Worcestershire.

Another view of the Rednal tram terminus, in 1952. The 200-yard-long terminal loop with its large curved wrought-iron shelter dated from 1925. A railed central garden gave the air of a popular resort to the terminus.

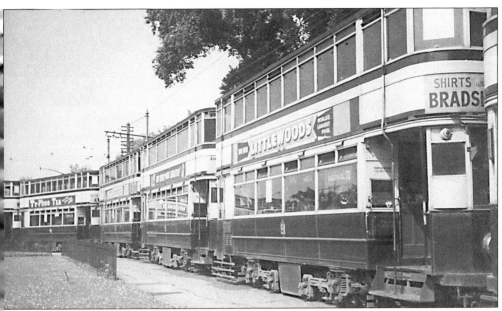

The grandiose terminal loop catered for the vast crowds of visitors travelling to the Lickeys at that time. In the summer months during the inter-war years, the Selly Oak depot could not meet the demand unaided, and extra cars were supplied by the Moseley Road depot. The terminal loop (seen here in 1952) was also used for stabling eighteen trams which exceeded capacity at Selly Oak.

Driver and conductress at Rednal terminus in 1952.

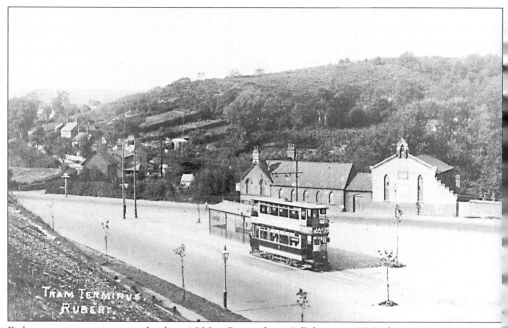

Rubery tram terminus in the late 1920s. Opened on 8 February 1926, the service terminated within the city boundary, outside the gates of Rubery Hill Hospital and close to Cock Hill Lane. The Rubery extension operated on reserved track, in common with most of the main Bristol Road service. Like the Rednal service, it lasted until 1952.

TIME TABLES.

BY TRAIN, New Street, Platform 6, to Barnt Green.
Fare 10½d.

A.M.—6.32, 6.41, 8.55, 9.50, 11.30.   P.M.—12.5*, 12.28,
12.42 ,1.10, 1.18†, 2.16*, 3.6, 3.15, 4.40, 5.0, 5.46,
6.12†, 6.21, 7.15, 7.25.

*Starts from Plat. 5.   †Saturdays only.

RETURN FROM BARNT GREEN.

A.M.—6.56, 7.44, 7.57, 8.36, 9.4, 9.12, 9.46, 10.24, 10.44,
11.49.   P.M—12.45, 1.31, 2.18, 3.24, 3.38, 3.51, 4.56,
5.12, 6.25, 7.12 7.28 8.32, 8.56, 9.10, 10.14.

SUNDAYS.

To Barnt Green.   A.M.—8.10, 8.45.   P.M.—4.27, 4.50,
5.50, 8.12, 8.50.

To Birmingham.   A.M.—9.36, 11.7.   P.M.—5.27, 8.49, 9.0,
9.22.

BY TRAM from Navigation Street to Rednal.   Fare 5d.

WEEK DAYS.

First Tram 9.30 a.m., and about every ten minutes to
last Tram, 11.30 p.m.
From Rednal. First Tram 10.30 a.m., last Tram 11.45 p.m.

SUNDAYS.

From Navigation Street. First Tram 9.30 a.m., and as
required to last Tram, 11.30 p.m.
From Rednal. First Tram 9.30 a.m., last Tram 10.45 p.m.

Train and tram timetables for Lickey Hills services, at the height of the tourist boom in 1924, when the train fare from Birmingham was less than 10½d (5p), and the tram fare half that.

The signal box at Rubery station, with a visiting goods train, in the 1930s. Rubery station stood at the bottom of Holly Hill, about half a mile from the village. It was served by the Longbridge to Halesowen Railway, which opened in 1883 as a joint venture between the Great Western and Midland companies.

Rubery station from Holly Hill Quarry, with Rubery Hill Hospital buildings on the skyline beyond, c. 1905. The railway sidings were laid out in 1902 to carry sand and stone from the quarry to the construction site at Frankley Reservoir. Apart from serving the needs of local residents and visitors to the hospital, the railway offered an alternative approach to the Lickeys for day trippers.

A general view of Rubery station in 1954. Hunnington, with its spectacular cast-iron trestle viaduct, was the other intermediate station on the line, which was single-track with passing loops. There were initially seven trains a day between Kings Norton and Halesowen, one being a through-train to New Street.

The signal box at Rubery station, 1954. The weight restriction on the Hunnington viaduct where speed was limited to 10mph, prevented the establishment of a fast and frequent service and the line was never a commercial success in spite of special workmen's services for the Longbridge car factory.

Rubery signal box and station, 1954. Regular passenger services ceased to run between Longbridge and Halesowen in April 1919, although workmen's specials continued to run until 1964.

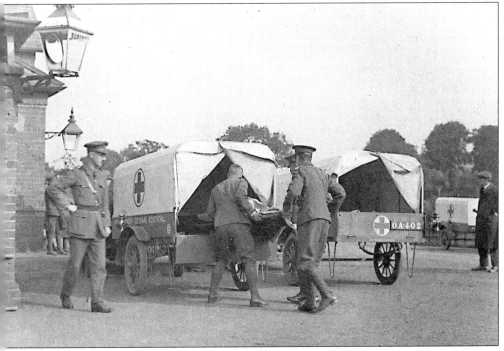

Loading trailers for the war hospitals at Rubery station, c. 1916. The station was probably most heavily used at this time, since there were several specially designated war hospitals in the area, including Rubery Hill and the University of Birmingham.

A surviving relic of the railway, the crossing keeper's lodge at Holly Hill, in the early 1970s.

The old railway track, looking east, in the early 1970s. Parts of the line passing through Rubery survive in the form of a footpath.

A steam train passing through Barnt Green station, *c.* 1930. Barnt Green is the oldest station of Birmingham's Cross City Line, having been in continuous use, on more or less the same site, since 17 September 1840. Formerly important for cattle and racing pigeon traffic, it once played host to the Royal Train; George VI slept in the siding one night in March 1938 before visiting the shadow (armaments) factory at Cofton. Close to Barnt Green station lies the famous Lickey Incline, which in the days of the steam train, could only be climbed with the aid of extra engines known as bankers.

A scene at Kendal End, Barnt Green, just round the corner from the station, with Bittell Road merging into Barnt Green Road (leading to Rednal) straight ahead, and a 1925 Standard emerging from Blackwell Road on the left. In this 1926 photograph, the railway bridge – forming a 'gateway' to Barnt Green village – carries the Birmingham-Gloucester line.

AUSTIN W

THE 12 H.P. WINDSOR SALOON.
Very smart, neat and attractive model with
many conveniences for comfort. Independent
adjustment for front seats. Four wide doors
and ample windows.

THE AUSTIN SEVEN.
A small touring car to seat two adults and two
children. Reliable, because designed for hard
service. Possesses every good quality of larger
cars.

A panoramic view of Herbert Austin's car factory, with the Lickey Hills in the background. This picture was published in the firm's short commemorative history, *The coming of age 1905-1926*, and showed four of their most notable popular and quality models. Famous for 'motorising the masses', Austin was a hands-on employer, priding himself on being able to do everything

From small beginnings – The Austin car factory in the year of its foundation (1905), in a still predominantly rural setting.

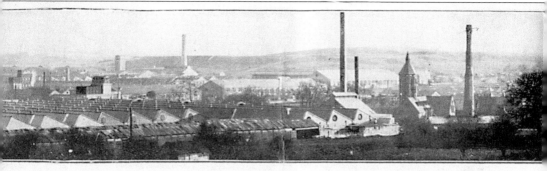

PRODUCTS.

THE 12 H.P. CLIFTON TOURING.
Economy, Strength, Docility and Capacity are the salient features of this model. Ample accommodation for five. Easy control. Four speeds and four wheel brakes.

THE 20 H.P. MAYFAIR LANDAULETTE.
Elegant and distinguished appearance. Generous accommodation for seven persons. Convertible to either chauffeur or owner driven. Silent, powerful, luxurious.

his workmen did. At this time, the works themselves covered an area of 62 acres, the total site (including the testing track) 220 acres, and there were over 8,000 workers. The firm had a large library, and extensive staff training, welfare and sporting facilities.

Herbert Austin driving the first car to be produced at his factory (1906). It was tested the same day on the Lickeys.

115

The end of the Lapal Tunnel at California, Bartley Green, c. 1900. The tunnel played a key role in the extension of the Dudley Canal at Netherton by way of Halesowen and Lapal to the Worcester and Birmingham Canal at Selly Oak. The extension was built 1793-1798 to bypass the congested canals of the Black Country, and when completed was nearly 11 miles long, including the 3,795 yard Lapal Tunnel, the fourth longest in England.

The Lapal Tunnel and California Inn, in 1913. The tunnel had no towpath, and boats were 'legged' through, with a man lying on his back and pushing with his feet against the roof. In the early years, boats took four hours to pass through the tunnel; but following the allowing of hired help at California this was reduced during the 1820s to three hours. In 1841, a steam pumping engine was introduced near the mouth of the tunnel, which combined with the use of stop locks at each end, created a current to help boats through. The pump was used effectively until 1914 but continued problems of subsidence and ventilation led to several prolonged closures and to the eventual abandonment of the tunnel.

Seven
Leisure and Sport

The canal at California Bridge, Bartley Green, in the 1920s.

Women cyclists at Four Ways, Rednal, c. 1905.

Walking through the bluebell glades of Cofton Woods in 1925.

Yachting on the Bittell Reservoir, Barnt Green, in 1957.

Enjoying the miniature railway at the York Jones Pleasure Grounds in Cofton Woods, *c.* 1950.

Cofton Wood Tearooms, *c.* 1950. York Jones' cafe and funfair were favourite features of the Lickey Hills during the first half of twentieth century.

The Old Rose and Crown, Rednal, *c.* 1905. Athough the house was at this time still the home of Alfred Wenham, and known as 'Lickey Hills', much of the estate, including Rednal Hill, was now available to the public.

The Old Rose and Crown, outwardly little changed, but now under its old name and returned to its old role as a hotel and restaurant, in the early 1960s. Just as the original coaching inn had been celebrated by Elihu Burritt (whose tribute was that of an early American tourist), so the later building was portrayed most favourably in *Merry hearts at Rednal* (1935), by local writer Marianne Hipkins. This romantic tale of the Lickey Hills also featured the Bilberry Hill tearooms, the funfair, and a moonlight walk through the woods.

121

Skiing on the Lickeys in 1965. Building on the lower slopes of Beacon Hill has limited such opportunities in recent years, but the suggestion a few years ago of building an artificial ski slope for the Lickeys has not materialised.

Works party at Bilberry Hill Tearooms in 1939. Apart from regularly catering for day trippers the tearooms were also popular for concerts, dances and receptions of many kinds. It was regular venue for Cadbury outings before the firm became too large.

Lickey Golf Course looking towards Beacon Hill, c. 1950. Opened in the early 1920s, the eighteen-hole municipal course – one of the first of its kind in the country – was laid out and donated by the Cadbury family, who persuaded the City of Birmingham to run it. The course is complemented by adjacent facilities for the playing of tennis, bowls and miniature golf. The Birmingham Civic Society's report *Recreation in the Lickey Hills* (1920) had envisaged the Rose and Crown estate as the main sporting quarter of the Lickeys, but their ambitious proposals for an open-air theatre, maze, and swimming pool near the hotel were never implemented.

The Hare and Hounds, Rednal, c. 1914. This is the only survivor of four pubs which formerly stood near the tram terminus. Beginning as a simple cottage-style inn, it acquired a Mock-Tudor front in the Edwardian era, and was substantially extended in the inter-war period. To the right of the picture may be seen conveyances for the convenience of visitors to the hills, and one of the open-topped buses which was used at this time to provide a link with the tram service at Selly Oak.

The Barracks Inn, Rednal, c. 1910. This building is just one of three pubs that are no longer in existence, the others being the White Lion and the Plough and Harrow. The Barracks clearly used to cater for the tourist market, with its attractive raised veranda allowing visitors to watch the world go by on Lickey Road. It was demolished in the 1920s, and the site – now levelled and excavated – is occupied by a large garage.

Lickey Scout Troup, photographed in 1918, in the grounds of Lickey Grange, the home of Herbert Austin, the patron of the troup. Lord Austin's private secretary, W.A. Howitt, was the scoutmaster; he lived in one of the wooden-fronted houses on Rose Hill, built by Austin for his senior staff. The scouts still meet regularly at their headquarters in the old schoolhouse opposite Lickey church.

Rednal festival, held in 1936.

Rubery Carnival, 1978.

ew Rose & Crown Hotel
RUBERY.

Arthur George : Proprie

Calling at the New Rose and Crown, Rubery, *c.* 1915.

The Cock Inn, Rubery, in the early 1970s, still a country inn before the major housir developments soon to come.

An all-male gathering at Rubery Social Club in the 1920s.

Walking over the fields to Frankley Beeches in the 1920s.

In October 1896, Alvechurch Parish Council decided to revive the ancient custom of beating the bounds, which had not been observed in the village since 1661. Walking the boundary entailed crossing much difficult terrain, some of it at points where Alvechurch met Barnt Green or Cofton Hackett. Since the boundary at one point passed under the Bittell Reservoir, the party were required to take to the water for part of their journey.

Refreshments taken at the Towers, Barnt Green, helped to sustain the party in their 1896 perambulation of the parish of Alvechurch. Although by this time a purely ceremonial activity before the days of ordnance surveys and parish maps, the yearly scrutiny of boundaries was regarded as essential for the safeguarding of land ownership and the avoidance of encroachment by default or design.